ELIZABETH

CELTIC TREE MAGIC

The Witches' Almanac, Ltd.

Address all inquiries and information to
THE WITCHES' ALMANAC, LTD.
P.O. Box 4067
Middletown, Rhode Island 02842

First Printing August 1996

Printed in the United States of America

Sometimes a tree tells you more
than can be read in books

—CARL G. JUNG

An Alphabet of Trees

This is a mystery story. The Celtic Druids of Western Europe and the British Isles employed a mystic system of thought based on trees and the human hand. By such means, and no one can tell quite how, the Druids found spiritual and poetic inspiration enabling them to create beauty and divine the future. Priests and poets held high positions in Celtic society. Training was long and arduous; the culture achieved of the highest order. The civilization of which we know so little may have existed as early as 1200 B.C.

The actual disciplines practiced by the Druids are lost to us. Only clues remain, for it was an oral tradition at the outset. Many centuries would pass before evidence was committed to written form. There followed still later a series of translations accompanied by the usual scholarly disputes, which continue to the present day.

In matters of imagination and divination, a poet may be the best guide. British poet Robert Graves sought to define the Celtic tree alphabet in his classic study, *The White Goddess: A Historical Grammar of Poetic Myth*. Each of the twenty characters — fifteen consonants and five vowels — represents a particular tree and in turn, relates to the thumb and four fingers of the hand. Graves remarks that he first came across the tree alphabet in 17th-century author Roderick O'Flaherty's *Ogygia,* where it was presented as "a genuine relic of Druidism." Graves continues: "I noticed almost at once that the consonants of this alphabet form a calendar of seasonal tree-magic, and that all the trees figure prominently in European folklore."

THE LUNAR CONSONANTS

Beth (Birch) **B**	December 24 to January 20
Luis (Rowan) **L**	January 21 to February 17
Nion (Ash) **N**	February 18 to March 17
Fearn (Alder) **F**	March 18 to April 14
Saille (Willow) **S**	April 15 to May 12
Uath (Hawthorn) **H**	May 13 to June 9
Duir (Oak) **D**	June 10 to July 7
Tinne (Holly) **T**	July 8 to August 4
Coll (Hazel) **C**	August 5 to September 1
Muin (Vine) **M**	September 2 to September 29
Gort (Ivy) **G**	September 30 to October 27
Ngetal (Reed) **NG**	October 28 to November 24
Ruis (Elder) **R**	November 25 to December 22

December 23rd is not ruled by any tree, for it is the "day" of the proverbial "year and a day," from the earliest documents in courts of law.

B

Beth

BIRCH

Few trees figure more prominently in the folklore of Northern Europe than the birch. Deemed sacred to Thor, Norse god of thunder and lightning, the birch symbolizes youth and springtime. It is one of the hardiest trees in the world; growing further north, and, with the rowan and the ash, higher up mountains than any other species. The birch is called "the tree of inception" with good reason. Not only does it self-sow, forming groves, but it is one of the earliest forest trees to put out leaves in spring.

An Old English folk-ballad titled *The Wife of Usher's Well* has a line: "And their hats were o' the birk," echoing a rural theme that souls returning from the dead decked themselves with branches plucked from the birch trees surrounding the gates of Paradise. The boughs were worn for protection lest the winds of Earth discover them and thwart their mission. Medieval art often depicts a ghostly presence as a figure arrayed in birch branches.

Its uncanny nature links the tree with witchcraft. Birch is the wood of broomsticks; flying transport to the sabbat gatherings. Oral tradition holds that witches anoint their birch rods with the words: "Away we go, not too high and not too low."

Siberian shamans may still seek the "magic mushroom" (the scarlet white-spotted fly agaric) in birch groves where it flourishes. Intoxicated by the ritually ingested mushrooms, shamans reach a state of ecstasy by climbing a birch tree and cutting nine notches in its crown.

Birch lore turns up in many cultures. The Dakota Sioux burn birch bark to discourage thunder spirits. Dutch farmers decorate a birch branch with red and white ribbons to safeguard horses in their stables. Scandinavians carry a young dried leaf for good luck on the first day of a new job. Basque witches use birch oil to anoint love candles. A bough on the roof protects a German home from lightning strikes. A birch grove guarded the house and land in colonial New England. Many sources claim that smoke rising from a fire of birch logs purifies the surroundings.

$$L$$

Luis

ROWAN

So potent is the flower or berry or wood of the rowan or witchwood or quicken or whicken-tree or mountain ash against the wiles of the elf-folk, that dairymaids use it for cream-stirrers and cowherds for a switch.

—WALTER DE LA MARE

The bright red berries of the mountain ash give this tree its Scottish name "rowan" from the Gaelic *rudha-an*, the red one. An older and more romantic name is *luisliu*, flame or delight of the eye. The scarlet berries also account for its growing high on mountains along with the birch, for birds feast on the berries and drop seeds in crevices at altitudes as high as 3000 feet where the tree springs up and flourishes. Although the most common name for the rowan is mountain ash, it has no botanical relation to the true ash save for a resemblance in its smooth grey bark and graceful ascending branches. Other names for the rowan are whitebeam, quicken and witch-wood, the later possibly derives from the Anglo-Saxon root *wic*, meaning pliable.

Scandinavian myths assign the rowan to Thor, god of thunder. All across Northern Europe it was the custom to plant rowan trees near farm buildings to gain the favor of Thor and insure safety for stored crops and animals from storm damage. A necklace of rowan beads enlivened the wearer and twigs were carried as protective charms.

Rowan figures prominently in Scottish folklore as a sure means to counteract evil intent. It was believed that a christened person need only touch a suspected witch with rowan wood in order to break a spell as the poet Allan Ramsay wrote:

> *Rowan tree and red thread,*
> *Will put witches to their speed.*

Yet, a century earlier, in the case of Margaret Barclay, such a charm was damning evidence. Brought to trial for witchcraft in the town of Irvine, Ayrshire, Scotland in 1618, her conviction was assured when a piece of rowan tied with red yarn was found in her possession.

Nion

ASH

Like the birch and the rowan, the ash tree thrives high up on exposed hills. The tree is easily recognized by its pure grey bark and large, spreading crown especially after its leaves have fallen. The ash comes to leaf as late as May and loses its leaves by early October.

The Greeks dedicated the ash tree to Poseidon, god of the sea, and sailors carried its wood as protection against the threat of drowning. The major spiritual significance of the ash tree comes from Northern Europe, where as *Yggdrasil*, the World Tree, it connects the underworld, earth and heaven. The ash is associated in Norse myths with Odin (Woden), supreme among gods, who sought to increase his wisdom with extreme suffering. It was on an ash tree that he hanged himself:

> *Nine whole nights on a wind-rocked tree,*
> *Wounded with a spear.*
> *I was offered to Odin, myself to myself,*
> *On that tree that none may ever know*
> *What root beneath it runs.*

This account is recorded in the *Elder Edda*, Icelandic poems dating from about the 10th century.

Ash keys, so-called because they resemble keys used in medieval locks, are the winged seed pods dispersed by winter winds to form new trees. They are of value as fertility charms. Ash is one of the few woods that will burn easily and steadily when still green. Divination fires are often of green ash.

The Norns, mistresses of fate, tend the World Ash Tree — *Yggdrasil*.

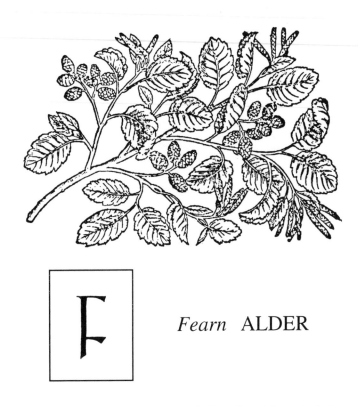

ᚠ *Fearn* ALDER

The first three trees of the alphabet flourish on heights and mountain slopes. By contrast, the alder is usually found thriving in thickets beside lakes, streams and rivers. It so favors marshy conditions that the tree seldom grows on drier land. Its black bark scored with cracks and broad oval leaves quickly identify the alder. As the timber dries after felling, its color changes from yellow to orange to red. When dried, the wood is water resistant and does not split when nailed. For centuries alder has provided pilings to serve as building founda-

tions throughout European lowlands. Charcoal derived from alder wood is superior to all others.

The alder is associated with Bran, a Celtic hero/god. One tale about him is found in the medieval Welsh collection of legends known as *The Mabinogion.* Another story, *The Voyage of Bran to the World Below*, occurs in Irish literature recorded in the 8th century. The sea-god Llyr (Welsh) and Lir (Irish) plays a role in both tales as do black birds: the starling, crow, and raven. The Irish epic describes Bran waking from a dream to find himself in the presence of a goddess and holding in his hand a silver branch. The branch magically springs from his hand to hers once he agrees to set sail for the abode of the goddess.

It is rare to find alder mentioned in European folklore. Old herbals, however, submit many practical uses for alder leaves.

Saille

WILLOW

Willows are magical trees with slender pale silver-green leaves. The weeping willow originated in China, where it graced cemeteries as a symbol of immortality, and the tree had spread to the Near East by Biblical times. An Old Testament reference to the exiled Jews hanging their harps upon the willows as they wept beside the rivers of Babylon led to the weeping willow's classification by Linnaeus as *Silax babylonica*. In ancient Greece, the goddess Hera was born under a willow on the island of Samos, where a magnificent temple was built to honor her. In the underworld kingdom of Pluto and Persephone, Orpheus touched a willow branch and received the gift of supernatural eloquence. Willow groves are sacred to Hecate, dark goddess of witchcraft.

During the Middle Ages, the willow became a traditional motif adorning tombs. Early 19th-century gravestones throughout New England were decorated with the willow emblem.

An old spell uses willow to dismiss love and transform passion into friendship.

At Full Moon snip a foot-long tendril from a weeping willow tree and braid it with equal lengths of bright red and cool green yarn. Tie three knots in the braid and hang the charm in an airy room until the Moon is in its last quarter. On three successive nights untie the knots one by one in privacy and silence while concentrating on your desire. Before the New Moon rises, burn the red strand to ashes and throw to the winds. Coil the willow and green wool together and place in an envelope for safe-keeping.

The willow of the Druids was not the weeping willow, but the tree or shrub we know as the pussy willow. The Irish called the pussy willow one of the "seven noble trees of the land."

The pussy willow is used in love charms as a guard against evil and its wands are often employed in divination. Reflecting the ancient status of the pussy willow, it is the wood to "knock on" and avert bad luck.

Medieval herbalists placed all willows under the rulership of the moon.

b | *Uath* HAWTHORN

The hawthorn is a small tree seldom exceeding 15 feet in height. Its long thorns provide protection against storm and grazing animals for larger trees like oak and ash that grow up beneath it and eventually supplant it. It also affords thorny shelter for birds and other wildlife that feast on its scarlet autumn berries. Although it grows well in most soils, the hawthorn prefers damp sandy earth for germination and is often a bird-sown tree. The bark is dark grey-brown and splits into a pattern of random squares with age. The flowers grow in clusters of white or palest pink and exude a strong unusual scent.

Hawthorn is so strongly associated with the Celtic May Eve festival that "may" is a folk name for it. Whitethorn is another name popular in Brittany, where the tree marks fairy trysting places. Sacred hawthorns guard wishing wells in Ireland, where shreds of clothing are hung on the thorns to symbolize a wish made. The Roman goddess Cardea, mistress of Janus who was keeper of the doors, had as her principal protective emblem a bough of hawthorn. "Her power is to open what is shut; to shut what is open."

Thorn trees are bewitched, according to old legends, and the hawthorn in particular caught the imagination of all Western Europe from earliest recorded time. In some cultures it served as a protection against lightning; in others it was thought to have purifying power. It was deemed the tree of chastity by the Old-Irish. Greek brides wore crowns of hawthorn blossoms in May, but Romans considered the month of May an inappropriate time to wed and the flowering hawthorn an ill omen, especially if brought inside the home. To the Turks, the hawthorn signified erotic desire. Mother Goose, in whose name so much of our folklore literature is preserved, yields a beauty secret:

The fair maid who, the first of May,
Goes to the fields at break of day,
And washes in dew from the hawthorn tree,
Will ever after handsome be.

Duir OAK

The first three trees of the Celtic alphabet—birch, rowan, ash—share a preference for high airy places. The next three—alder, willow, hawthorn—have strong associations with water. The seventh tree, the oak, grows everywhere.

Oaks grow taller and live longer than most other species of tree. Depending on the variety, oaks may range in height from 40 to 120 feet. An average life span is 250 years but there are oaks in England's Windsor Great Park reckoned to be over one thousand years old. The leaf form varies, as does the bark, but only the oak tree bears acorns.

Long held sacred, the oak was dedicated by the Greeks to Zeus, the Romans to Jupiter, and the Norsemen to Thor—all gods of the lightning flash. The Celtic priests of Britain and Gaul, the Druids, so revered the oak that their teachings and many spiritual rites were carried out in its shade. The veneration may derive from the fact that the acorn, fruit of the oak, was once a main food source to the wandering tribes of prehistoric Europe. The acorn in mystic lore represents the highest form of fertility—creativity of the mind.

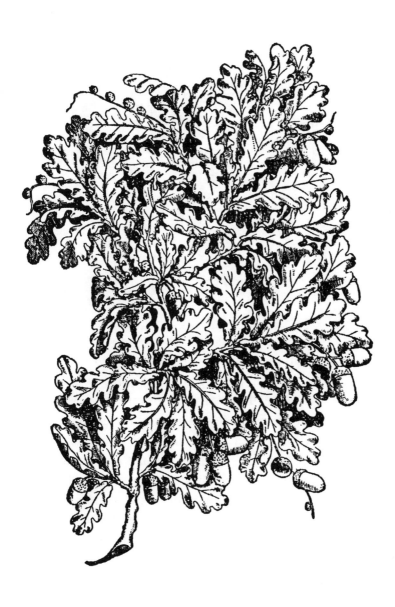

T

Tinne

HOLLY

Some occultists place yew as the eighth tree representing the consonants in the tree alphabet of the Druids. Others, however, call for holly to follow the oak. This sequence accords with many folktales and celebrations that present the oak and holly trees as two Divine Kings, one representing the waxing half of the year when the sun rises to its height at summer solstice, the other as symbol of the waning cycle as the sun retreats to its lowest point at midwinter solstice. The Celtic myth of Sir Gawain and the Green Knight has the two opponents meeting in combat at midsummer and midwinter. Gawain carries a club of oak. The Green Knight's weapon is a bough of holly.

Holly is an evergreen growing as an under-shrub in many woods and forests. Some varieties given space and opportunity will grow to be 40 feet tall. The waxy surface of its thick leaves enables the holly to resist water loss when the soil is frozen. The dark green lower leaves have sharp spines which discourage browsing animals during the winter months. The holly is either male or female and both bear flowers, but the female flowers develop into bright red berries in autumn. Country wisdom advises that one should always plant a pair of hollies to allow for cross-fertilization. A barren holly is regarded as unlucky.

The oak, ash and holly were favored trees in the sacred groves of the Druids. The holly had a strong association with divination in Northern Europe. A charm to bring a dream of your future mate required nine spiky leaves of holly collected at midnight before moonrise. Complete silence was to be observed as you wrapped the leaves in a square of pure white linen, placed the packet under your pillow and dreamed the night away.

The Romans decorated their homes with boughs of holly during the December festival of Saturnalia; Mediterranean "holly" comes from the evergreen kermes or holly oak with a leaf form identical to the true holly of the north. This tree, too, was credited with magical power. Pliny, in the 1st century A.D., wrote, "A holly tree planted in a town house or a country house keeps off uncanny influences."

C

Coll

HAZEL

Nine is a magic number and the ninth consonant of the Druid's alphabet belongs to the tree of wisdom, poetic art, and divination—the magical hazel tree.

Unprepossessing to look at, more a spreading bush than a tree, the hazel rarely exceeds 12 feet in height. Bright brown bark mottled with grey, male and female catkins hanging like tassels, and oval leaves with toothed edges are identifying marks of the hazel. Hazel thickets provide winter cover for wildlife. Its branches in time past served as fences, pea poles, clothes props, and secured thatch for roofs of cottages.

Excellent kindling wood, the hazel was the first choice of bakers for their ovens.

The magical significance of hazel crosses cultural lines, for it appears in the lore of Northern and Southern Europe and the Near East. The staff of the Roman god Mercury was of hazel wood. The myths say Apollo presented the caduceus to Hermes, the Greek counterpart of Mercury, in recognition of his mystical power to calm human passion and improve virtue. The medieval magician's wand was traditionally cut from the hazel tree with scrupulous ceremony drawn from Hebraic sources. Ancient Irish heralds carried white hazel wands. The "wishing rods" of Teutonic legend were cut from the hazel tree.

Hazel's function as a divining tool is many centuries old. The forked hazel-stick employed by dowsers to discover underground water sources, mineral deposits, and buried treasure is still in use today as it was before the turn of the Christian era.

Hazelnuts, often called filberts, are used as charms to promote fertility. Charles Godfrey Leland says "a rosary of hazelnuts brings good luck when hung in a house, and hazelnut necklaces found in prehistoric tombs were probably amulets as well as ornaments." Hazelnuts turn up in a variety of forms of love divination: share a double nut with someone you love and if silence is maintained while the nuts are eaten, your love will grow.

Muin

VINE

Celtic scholars now agree that the "vine" of the Druidic tree alphabet refers to the blackberry bramble bush. The sacred nature of the blackberry is evidenced in old tales and heathen customs observed down through the centuries. A loop of blackberry bramble served as a healing source in much the same way as a holed stone. Traditional rites involved passing a baby through the loop three times to secure good health. One ancient legend tells how blackberries gathered and eaten within the span of the waxing moon at harvest time assured protection from the force of evil runes. For refuge in times of danger, one need only creep under a bramble bush. In rural regions of France and the British Isles, even to the present day, it is considered dangerous to eat blackberries. The reason given in Brittany is that the fruit belongs to the fairies and they resent it when mere mortals presume to taste the magical berries.

Blackberry is one of the few plants bearing blossoms and fruit at the same time. Its curative values were many and recognized in medieval herbals. A major virtue was its reputed power to lift the spirits by restoring energy and hope. This theme persisted, for in Victorian England physicians often prescribed blackberry cordial to cheer a depressed patient.

A clue to blackberry magic may be found in a nugget of country wisdom. When frozen dew covers blackberry blossoms at dawn in early spring, farmers rejoice and hail the event as a "blackberry winter." Without this frost, the berries will not set. What may appear threatening turns out to be a blessing, for the hoarfrost is a harbinger of a rich harvest.

 *Gort* IVY

When ivy trails along the ground it remains weak and
does not produce fruit, but when it climbs using a tree
or a wall for support, it grows increasingly stronger
putting out flowers in autumn and berries in the spring.
Birds feast on ivy's purple-black berries scattering the

seeds to form new plants in the soft spring earth. Ivy draws no nourishment from the tree it climbs nor do its underground roots seriously compete with the tree's roots for nutrients in the soil. Ivy growing up the walls of buildings promotes dryness within and serves as a protective shield against the atmosphere. Its botanical name in Latin is *Hedera helix* and describes ivy's spiral form of growth, for *helix* means "to turn round."

The rich deep evergreen color and climbing spiral action inspired the ancients to identify ivy with immortality, resurrection and rebirth. The classical gods of wine, the Greek Dionysos and his Roman counterpart Bacchus, are often depicted wearing crowns of ivy. This association with the grapevine, which also grows in spiral form, gave ivy the reputation for diminishing drunkenness, for it was thought that one spiral reversed the power of the other. Ivy came to symbolize fidelity and one perfect leaf collected when the moon was one day old was a useful amulet in matters of love.

Ngetal

REED

Following the sequence of the tree alphabet, we descend from the highest mountain to sea level, for the reed thrives in streams and marshes. Its other names—marsh-elder and guelder-rose—reveal an affinity for Europe's low-lying coastal regions, especially Holland. "Guelder" refers to Gelderland, a Dutch province bordering the Zuider Zee.

The reed reaches a height of 10 to 15 feet, comes to creamy white bloom in June and is harvested in November to provide thatching for cottage roofs. The herbalist Gerard in 1597 remarked on the beauty of its flowers and lamented its lack of fruit.

The folklore of Northern Europe has little regard for the reed, other than as a water-loving plant through which the winds play and may make sounds that convey esoteric messages. But in more sun-kissed regions, reeds — slender and delicate, steadfast and useful — play significant roles in various myths and symbols.

In ancient Egypt, the tropical canna reed inspired the design of the royal scepter, and arrows cut from its stalk were symbols of the pharaoh's power. In Greece, another variety of reed played a role in Pan's pursuit of the lovely chaste Syrinx. Pan pursued the nymph from mountain to river, where she eluded him by becoming a reed. The god, bewildered by the myriad reeds and unable to recognize Syrinx among them, cut several of the plants at random — and out of these, to turn his lust and sorrow into song, devised the glorious panpipe.

Metamorphosis turns up frequently in ancient Greek stories, especially the theme of maidens transforming into trees to avoid violation. Pan seemed particularly luckless in the sexual chase, and according to myth nymphs would go to any lengths to avoid his embrace. He was similarly thwarted by Pitys, who became a fir tree to escape his attentions. Resigned, this time the god made the best of his loss by cutting a branch and making a crown of the fir, which he wore ever after.

Even the great god Apollo, celebrated for his beauty and musical magic, sometimes failed to win his heart's desire. According to the Roman poet Ovid in his *Metamorphosis*, Daphne became a bay laurel tree rather than submit to the god's embrace.

Ruis

ELDER

Diana of Ephesus was originally worshipped in the form of a date palm, and the elder tree of Northern Europe once had a similar resident deity whose magical significance has lasted through the centuries. Scandinavian legends tell of the Elder Mother who watches for any injury to the tree. If even a sprig is cut without first asking permission of the Elder Mother, whatever purpose the sprig is cut for will end in misfortune.

Once permission has been asked and a twig of the elder secured, it will banish evil spirits and may be hung or worn as an amulet. Elder flowers, dried while the moon waxes from dark to full, are a potent love charm. The berries gathered at summer solstice afford protection from all unexpected dangers, including accidents and lightning strikes.

Beyond its subtle gifts, the elder offers healing for a variety of ailments. Its leaves are an effective insect repellent; its close-grained wood finds favor with carpenters; its berries provide a deep purple dye as well as culinary treats and the renowned elderberry wine.

Reverence for the Elder Mother challenged the early Christian church fathers and soon missionary priests redefined the tree goddess as a wicked witch more to be feared than adored. Moreover, Judas, betrayer of Christ, hanged himself on an elder tree, and Christ was crucified on a cross of elder. To place a baby in an elder cradle invited an evil spirit to come and snuff out its life. The tree constituted so serious a threat that England's King Edgar in the 10th century issued a warning against "those vain practices which are carried on with Elders."

Folklore passed down to us today reflects these ambivalent attitudes, for elder is more often considered evil than good. Only in Denmark has the Elder Mother, *Hylde-Moer*, retained her sacred nature. Hans Christian Andersen's tale of the Elder Mother who becomes a beautiful maiden named Memory captures the spirit of the most ancient lore.

Although the elder likes moist soil, it grows everywhere if sheltered from the wind.

It isn't clear why the last two consonants of the tree alphabet are omitted from the seasonal calendar. Robert Graves suggests that the blackthorn may share a month with the willow, because it blooms in early spring. And as the apple and hazelnut harvest coincide, both trees share a month as well.

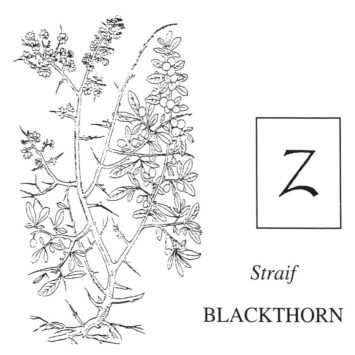

Straif

BLACKTHORN

With a name denoting darkness and pain, the blackthorn was considered unlucky and its wood identified as the staff of sorcerers. Other than that, the blackthorn or sloe rates little attention in folk legends and herbal lore. Curiously, the French call it *Mother of the Wood*.

And in a lovely Irish folk song, the blackthorn (*An Droighnean Donn*) is more admired than feared:

By road and by river the wild birds sing,
O'er mountain and valley the dewy leaves spring,
The gay flowers are shining, gilt o'er by the sun,
And fairest of all shines the blackthorn.

The rath of the fairy, the ruin hoar,
With white silver splendour it decks them all o'er;
And down in the valleys, where merry streams run,
How sweet smells the bloom of the blackthorn!

Ah! Well I remember the soft spring day,
I sat by my love 'neath its sweet-scented spray;
The day that she told me her heart I had won,
Beneath the white blossoms of the blackthorn.

The streams they were singing their gladsome song,
The soft winds were blowing the wild woods among,
The mountains shone bright in the red setting sun,
And my love in my arms 'neath the blackthorn.

—ROBERT DWYER JOYCE

Quert

APPLE

More than any other fruit, the apple plays a significant role in many ancient love stories. The Greek myths tell of a wondrous orchard of golden apples, a wedding gift from the Earth Mother, Gaea, to Hera upon her marriage to Zeus. The apple trees grew in the far west, where the sun sets and the evening star appears. The Hesperides, the three daughters of Atlas and the Darkness of Night, were custodians of the orchard. Acquiring the golden apples was one of the labors assigned to Hercules in his quest for redemption. Venus won a golden apple as prize for being the fairest of goddesses, as judged by the bewitched eyes of Paris. The German love goddess is portrayed as carrying an apple to the May-Eve revels.

Little wonder that folklore collections contain a myriad of love charms using the apple from peel to seed. Welsh legends link apples and immortality, for kings and heroes adjourned after death to Avalon, an island paradise of apple trees where their youth and vigor were restored. Scandinavian myths tell of gods who kept themselves eternally young by partaking of the apples kept in a chest by Iduna, goddess of youth and renewal. Health-giving properties of the apple rejuvenated mortals as well. Cut an apple in half crosswise and you see a five-pointed star, the pentagram, an ancient symbol of well being. Love, immortality, and vitality are the magic gifts of the apple tree.

An imaginative translation of the Old Testament made the apple the "forbidden fruit" in the Garden of Eden. The original text describes the tree only as possessing "the knowledge of good and evil." Association with a serpent, sin, shame and lust failed to diminish the popularity of the apple.

A memory of the esteem held by the tree comes from *The Triads* of ancient Ireland, where "three unbreathing things paid for only with breathing things: an apple tree, a hazel bush, a sacred grove." Irish mystic tradition defined the pursuit of wisdom as a quest to find a white doe under a wild apple tree.

Apple trees thrive in cool climates where winter temperatures average below 48 degrees.

The consonants of the alphabet of trees represent the thirteen lunar cycles occurring over the course of a year. All the trees chosen to represent them reflect the mystery and magic of the moon. Hidden aspects, lost secrets, the wondrous beauty of the night are qualities fleetingly perceived, if at all.

The significance of the vowels and their tree equivalents is as clearly defined as a landscape on a bright sunny day. With the possible exception of the yew, which was indeed a sacred object in European myths, the vowel trees hold no mystic meaning. They would seem to be no more than visible expressions of the seasons they herald. Pure and simple, the vowels mark the passage of the sun in its waxing and waning phases during a year of time.

THE SOLAR VOWELS

Ailm (Silver Fir) **A**   Winter Solstice

Onn (Furze) **O**   Spring Equinox

Ura (Heather) **U**   Summer Solstice

Eadha (Aspen) **E**   Autumnal Equinox

Idho (Yew) **I**   Winter Solstice

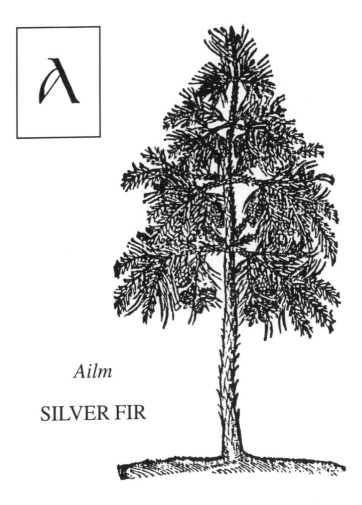

Ailm

SILVER FIR

Most appropriate is the choice of the silver fir to symbolize the dawn following winter solstice. A towering evergreen with a fiery red trunk in a bleak and snowy landscape points heavenward to mark the outset of the sun's journey back to northern climes.

O

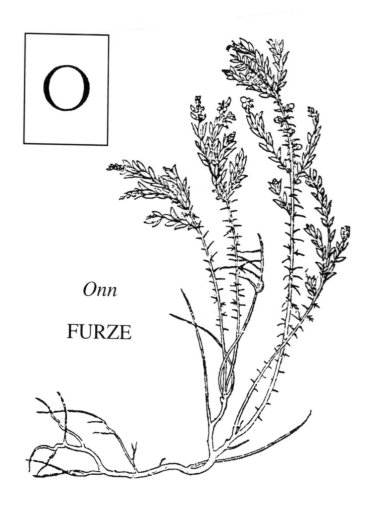

Onn

FURZE

The bright flowers of furze blanket hills, heaths and meadows to welcome spring equinox when the day and night are of equal length. Gold is the color of the sun and it is fitting that nature provides abundant yellow blossoms to greet the lush season of growing things.

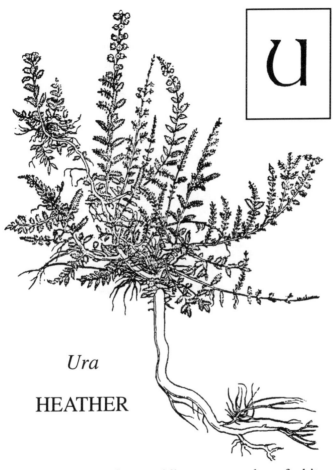

Ura

HEATHER

Heather now joins furze, adding great patches of white, pink and mauve flowers to the countryside's splendor; a visual tribute to summer solstice. At midsummer, the longest day of the year, the sun reaches the height of its power. Heather thrives in full sun and blooms through early autumn.

 *Eadha* ASPEN

Aspen leaves tremble in the lightest wind as if in warning of the chill weather soon to envelop the land. Autumnal equinox, when day and night are once again in perfect balance, marks the beginning of the sun's final retreat. The aspen or white poplar is a perfect emblem of anxiety.

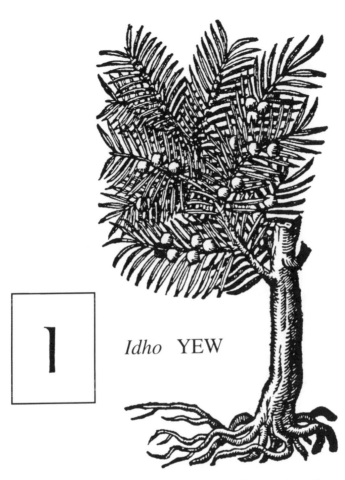

1

Idho YEW

The yew tree signifies both death and longevity. Yew groves favored by Druids became over time the sites of Christian churches and their adjoining cemeteries. As the weak sun sets on the eve of winter solstice, the yew is not only symbolic of the death of the year, but a promise of rebirth.

The Hand and the Trees

In time past, the human hand was regarded with deep reverence. The ancient Greeks and Romans identified each finger with a particular deity, and many European customs and ceremonies of later centuries found precedence in the classical system of correspondences. Older still and of unknown origin is the tradition that the left palm reveals the basic character of a person, while the lines on the right palm show how destiny is modified by choice and the exercise of free will. The reading of hands became the art of palmistry, a skill practiced throughout the world. The seers of Ireland — the Celts and their predecessors — were unique in the way they chose to use the hand as an oracle.

The Druids linked every finger joint and tip with a letter and its tree symbol. The colloquial expression "to have at one's fingertips" meaning "to be thoroughly acquainted with" relates to an Old-Irish rite called *dichetal do chennaib*, to recite from the finger-ends. The tips of the fingers were evidently used in such a manner as to induce a divinatory trance in prelude to uttering prophesy and poetry. The Druidic scheme of finger symbols offers an opportunity for intriguing speculation. Touch may be the most neglected of senses.

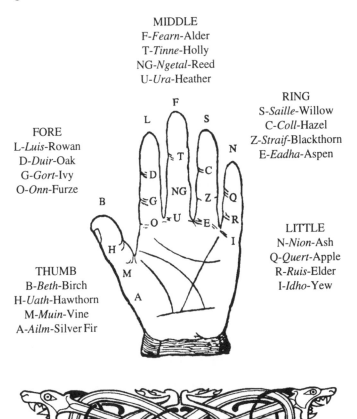

MIDDLE
F-*Fearn*-Alder
T-*Tinne*-Holly
NG-*Ngetal*-Reed
U-*Ura*-Heather

RING
S-*Saille*-Willow
C-*Coll*-Hazel
Z-*Straif*-Blackthorn
E-*Eadha*-Aspen

FORE
L-*Luis*-Rowan
D-*Duir*-Oak
G-*Gort*-Ivy
O-*Onn*-Furze

LITTLE
N-*Nion*-Ash
Q-*Quert*-Apple
R-*Ruis*-Elder
I-*Idho*-Yew

THUMB
B-*Beth*-Birch
H-*Uath*-Hawthorn
M-*Muin*-Vine
A-*Ailm*-Silver Fir

THE THUMB

Inception is its theme. B for Birch, the first letter of the tree alphabet, belongs to the tip of the thumb. The first joint is hawthorn, the May tree of love and sexuality, signifying the creative force of nature. Joyful anticipation is the keynote of the blackberry bush and bramble. A, the vowel at the base of the thumb, is the silver fir of winter solstice marking the moment when the sun begins its annual return to the northern hemisphere.

THE FOREFINGER

Symbolizing both lunar and solar realms, the forefinger's tip is named for the magical rowan tree and its first joint for the sacred oak. Such a combination gives the forefinger power beyond all others. The ivy suggests endurance and fidelity. Furze, ritually burned each spring to promote new growth, is an emblem for the vernal equinox, the start of spring.

THE MIDDLE FINGER

The Roman historian Pliny noted that the Celts wore rings on their middle fingers, a custom practiced by neither the Greeks nor the Romans, for in their culture it was the finger of disgrace.Conversely, Druidic lore identifies the middle finger with change and renewal. The alder tip is strongly associated with Bran, Celtic

Celtic raven god/hero. Holly, akin to the first joint, is borne by the Green Knight, or Fool, who in medieval holiday pageants was beheaded but rose unharmed. The reed typifies flexibility and movement. Heather, sign of the summer solstice, is the time of year when the sun begins its retreat and the days grow shorter.

THE RING FINGER

The custom of wearing a wedding ring on the third finger of the left hand arose because it was believed that an artery ran directly from it to the heart, source of everlasting love. The Druidic classification is far more subtle. The tip belongs to the willow, mysterious emblem of the moon's power of enchantment. Hazel is renowned as a source of spiritual wisdom. Perhaps ominous, certainly obscure is the meaning of the blackthorn. Autumnal equinox suits the quaking aspen.

THE LITTLE FINGER

All the fingertip trees of the Druidic alphabet are divinatory in nature. The little finger's tip corresponds to the highly regarded ash tree. The wild apple tree, the little finger's first joint, is a poet's symbolic passport to paradise. The mystic connotations of the sacred elder tree are legendary. And finally yew, the tree of death, for now the sun has run its course at winter solstice— the longest night of the year.

Poetry and the Spirit

When 9th-century Irish monks were forced to flee Ireland to escape the ravages of Viking raids, they found sanctuary in the monasteries of the continent. Their works, beautifully inscribed on vellum, became Church treasures and are preserved to this day in many European countries. Often in the margins of these old manuscripts are to be found scraps of poetry written in Gaelic. And it was these fragments that originally inspired a German linguist to begin to collect and translate them.

Kuno Meyer, scholar and philologist, gave the world a great gift with the publication of his *Ancient Irish Poetry* in the early years of the 20th century. In his Introduction, Dr. Meyer tells us that "these poems occupy a unique position in the literature of the world. To seek out and watch and love Nature, in its tiniest phenomena as in its grandest, was given to no other people so early and so fully as to the Celt. Many hundreds of Gaelic and Welsh poems testify to this fact. It is a characteristic of these poems that in none of them do we get an elaborate or sustained description of any scene or scenery, but rather a succession of pictures and images which the poet, like an impressionist, calls up before us by light and skillful touches. Like the Japanese, the Celts were always quick to take an artistic hint; they avoid the obvious and the commonplace; the half-said thing to them is dearest."

Unless otherwise credited, the poems that follow are from the translations by Kuno Meyer.

It has been said that the Old-Irish poets composed their works in darkness. Insight and inspiration might be summoned by three magical means: *teinm laida* (illumination by sound), *imbas forosna* (illumination by dream), and *dichetal do chennaib* (illumination by touch).

SUMMER IS COME

Summer is come, healthy free,
That bows down the dark wood;
The slim, spry deer leap,
And the path of seals is smooth.

The cuckoo sings sweet music,
And there is smooth, soft sleep.
Gentle birds skim the quiet hill
And the swift grey stags.

The deer's lair is too hot,
And active packs cry pleasantly.
The white stretch of strand smiles
And the swift sea grows rough.

There is a sound of wanton winds
In the tops of Drum Daill's black oakwood;
The fine clipped horses who shelter
In Cuan-wood are rushing about.

Green bursts out from every plant;
Leafy is the shoot of the green oakwood,
Summer is come, winter gone,
Twisted hollies wound the hound.

The hardy blackbird who owns
The thorny wood sings a bass;
The wild and weary sea reposes
And the speckled salmon leaps.

Over every land the sun smiles
For me a parting greeting to winter.
Hounds bark, stags tryst,
Ravens flourish, summer is come!

THREE CHARMS

Today I gird myself with the strength of heaven,
The light of the sun, the brilliance of the moon,
The glory of fire, the impetuousity of lightning,
The speed of the wind, the profundity of the sea,
The stability of earth, the hardness of rock.

> *I call on the seven daughters of the sea,*
> *who shape the threads of long life:*
> *Three deaths be taken from me,*
> *Three lives given to me,*
> *Seven waves of plenty poured for me.*

May my seven candles not be quenched.
I am an invincible fortress, I am an unshakable cliff,
I am a precious stone, I am the symbol of seven riches,
I summon my good fortune to me.

FOUR WINDS

When the wind sets from the east
The spirit of the wave is stirred.
It longs to rush past us westward
To the land over which the sun sets,
To the green sea, rough and wild.

When the wind sets from the north,
It urges the dark fierce waves,
Surging in strife against the wide sky,
Listening to the witching song.

When the wind sets from the west,
Over the salt sea of swift currents,
It longs to go past us eastward
To capture the Sun-Tree
In the wide, far-distant sea.

When the wind sets from the south,
Over the land of the Saxons of stout shields
And the wave strikes the isle of Scit,
It surges up to the top of Calad Net
With a leafy, grey-green cloak.

Development of memory is essential in a culture recorded only by oral tradition. Units of three are easy to remember.

THE TRIADS OF IRELAND

Three candles that illume every darkness: truth, nature, knowledge.

The three great ends of knowledge: duty, utility, decorum.

Three things that ruin wisdom: ignorance, inaccurate knowledge, forgetfulness.

Three things that corrupt the world: pride, superfluity, indolence.

Three things that come unbidden: fear, jealousy, love.

Three keys that unlock thoughts: drunkenness, trustfulness, love.

Three rude ones of the world: a youngster mocking an old man, a robust person mocking an invalid, a wise man mocking a fool.

Three sisters of youth: desire, beauty, generosity.

Three sparks that kindle love: a face, demeanor, speech.

Three laughing-stocks of the world: an angry man, a jealous man, a niggard.

Three excellences of dress: elegance, comfort, lastingness.

Three signs of a rogue: bitterness, hatred, cowardice.

Songs come down unwritten from mother to daughter.
This may be one of the oldest in existence.

LULLABY OF A WOMAN OF THE MOUNTAIN

O little head of gold! O candle of my house!
Thou wilt guide all who travel this country.

Be quiet, O house! and O little grey mice,
Stay at home tonight in your hidden lairs!

O moths on the window, fold your wings!
Cease your droning, O little black chafers!

O plover and O curlew, over my house do not travel!
Speak not O barnacle-goose, going over the
mountain, here!

O creatures of the mountain, that wake so early,
Stir not tonight till the sun whitens over you!

Songs of Sleep and of Sorrow
Translation by Thomas MacDonagh

Most of the old lyrics were found here and there in Europe, written on the margins of grammars and bibles, or assembled, a few together, in books of miscellany. Others may be discovered in the prose sagas and histories of early Irish literature. In the tales of Finn, the Ossianic Cycle, the hero proves his poetic skill with this lay:

> *May-day, season surpassing!*
> *Splendid is color then.*
> *Blackbirds sing a full lay,*
> *If there be a slender shaft of day.*
>
> *The dust-colored cuckoo calls aloud:*
> *Welcome, splendid summer!*
> *The bitterness of bad weather is past,*
> *The boughs of the wood are a thicket.*
>
> *The harp of the forest sounds music,*
> *The sail gathers — perfect peace;*
> *Color has settled on every height,*
> *Haze on the lake of full waters.*

Cailte, the chief poet of the Fianna, a warrior band who guarded Ireland's High King, describes the quality of his lord:

Were but the brown leaf,
Which the wood sheds from it, gold,
Were but the white billow silver,
Finn would have given it all away.

And one snowy November eve, Cailte said:

Winter is cold; the wind has risen;
The fierce stark-wild stag arises;
Not warm tonight is the unbroken mountain,
Even though the swift stag be belling.

Acallam na Senorach, Colloquy of Ancient Men.
Translation by Standish H. O'Grady

In The Battle of Moytura, the multi-gifted Lugh of the Tuatha De Danann plans a defense against the rampaging Fomorians:

"And ye, O Be-Culle and O Dianann," said Lugh to his two witches, "what power can ye wield in the battle?"

"Not hard to tell," said they. "We will enchant the trees and the stones and the sods of the earth, so that they shall become a host under arms against them, and shall rout them in flight with horror and trembling."

Ancient Irish Tales
Translation by Cross and Slover

The Tuatha De Danann triumphed and ruled Ireland for many centuries until the coming of the Milesians. The most often quoted ancient poem was spoken by Amergin, the bard of the invading force, as he set his right foot on Ireland's shore.

THE SONG OF AMERGIN

I am a stag of seven tines.
I am a lake in a plain.
I am a wind of the sea.
I am a dewdrop in the sun.
I am a hawk on a cliff.
I am fair among flowers.
I am the mind's fire of inspiration.
I am a battle-waging spear.
I am a salmon in a pool.
I am the strength of art.
I am a boar for valor.
I am the roar of the sea.
I am a wave of the ocean.